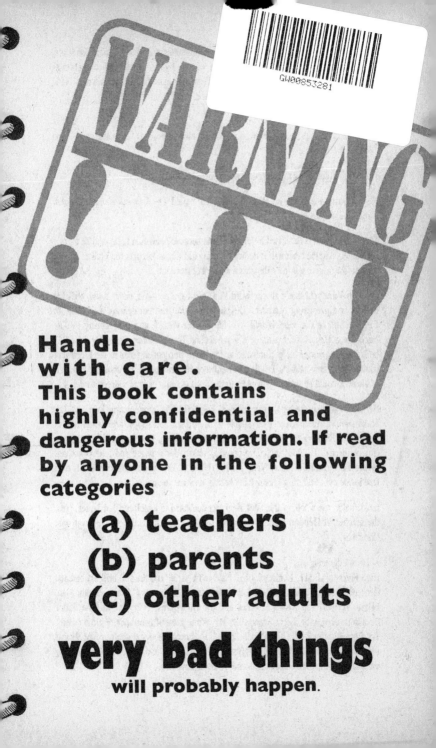

WARNING

Handle with care. This book contains highly confidential and dangerous information. If read by anyone in the following categories

(a) teachers
(b) parents
(c) other adults

very bad things
will probably happen.

Tim de Jongh is a writer and actor whose work includes *And Now In Colour* on Radio 4, and its recent BBC 2 pilot: *It's A Mad World, World, World, World*. He was President of the Cambridge Footlights in 1987 and is a qualified Drama teacher. He is also a member of the R.A.C. Breakdown Service.

Here are three complete lies about him:

If the letters 'Tim de Jongh' are rearranged they make the words 'aaaaaaaaaaargh', and 'Wisbeach Chronicle'

He is 14th in line to be manager of a well known bicycle repair shop.

He has written a smash hit West End musical called *The Kenneth Kendal Kenneth Kendal Kenneth Kendal Hopping Show*.

Half of this book is dedicated to James Knight because I saw him today and he's got a broken leg, and the other half is dedicated to my old school teachers Mr Walker and Mr Macintosh for giving us all a disastrous amount of freedom.

William Vandyck, that's all one word Van-*d-y-c-k* no, not – oh, never mind, NEVER MIND, is a practising barrister. Despite co-writing and performing *And Now, In Colour*, and *It's A Mad World, World, World, World*, and performing in *The Intelligence Men*, *A Kitchenette of Composers* and *The Legendary Series* for the BBC, he is best known for his performance as the bloke who pulled faces in the Electrolux commercials, and 'Man At Till' in *The Return of Mr Bean* where his shoulder and a bit of his neck could be seen (if you had a freeze frame facility on your video recorder).

He has co-written the highly somethinged *Tony and Cleo's Interesting Year* and *The Musketeers Adventure Agency* available from brilliant bookshops, and would like to write *Face Painting for Morons* (for adults) and *The Lion, The Witch and The Moron* (for children). Hobbies include promoting international peace and understanding, saving the world from Alien Warlord DEATHBRINGERS and trying to push his own face inside out. Still, that's enough about him, how are you doing?

Incidentally, the whole of this book is in fact dedicated to Kathleen Eleri James, (yes, the teacher at Hendon Central!) for not thinking up an excuse fast enough last Christmas.

Acknowledgments
High Fives to: Eddie, Louise, Sophie, Kate and Charlie, and the still brilliant parents; George and Ines Turner; D, S, P, J & T Hutchinson; J, P, N & C Martin-Smith; Sian, Eilian, Hywell and Rhian Jameses and the Llewelyns; everyone at One Paper Buildings, obviously; Lissa Evans still; The White Lion of Mortimer, Finsbury Park; Ted from Romford; Mr Clive Priddle; Zurich in general; the legal genius of AEW and IWSDJHAGLAJHRJLBMPNBLW; Sonic; Tim and Mike. Oh, and Lucy Ogden NVQ and Rebecca Elgar for being patient and not always rubbish.

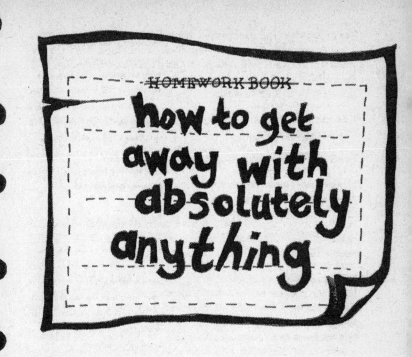

HOMEWORK BOOK

how to get away with absolutely anything

by

William Vandyck
& Tim de Jongh

A Catalogue record for
this book is available
from the British Library
ISBN 0-340-57287-6

Printed and bound in Great Britain for
Hodder and Stoughton Children's Books, a
division of Hodder and Stoughton Ltd, Mill
Road, Dunton Green, Sevenoaks, Kent
TN13 2YA (Editorial Office: 47 Bedford
Square, London WC1B 3DP) by Cox &
Wyman.

CONTENTS

THIS BOOK WILL CHANGE YOUR LIFE!

FOR A START YOU WILL HAVE SLIGHTLY LESS MONEY IF YOU BUY IT! (OR HAVE BOUGHT IT ALREADY.) THOUGH OBVIOUSLY IT'S WORTH IT! IF YOU STEAL IT, ON THE OTHER HAND, YOU BECOME LIABLE TO CRIMINAL PROSECUTION!

I SUPPOSE YOU COULD JUST LEAVE IT ALONE, BUT THEN YOU WOULD MISS OUT ON THE MOST FABULOUS OPPORTUNITY BECAUSE – HANG ON A SECOND – CAN WE STOP THE CAPITALS AS I'M GETTING A BIT OUT OF BREATH?

Thank you. Ooh, that's better.

If you don't get this book, you will miss out on the opportunity to take control of your life.

As you know, there are loads of emergencies that happen to you every day. Suddenly and without warning, you need money, or you need an excuse for being late, or not to do your homework, or you want to avoid washing up, or to stay up late.

Here, *now*, are the excuses to back you up in those emergencies and many others. Here, *now*, are the ideas to save you. Here, *now*, are things you can use against people you don't like, to make them (within certain socially acceptable limits and with all proper sensitivity) look stupid.

All sorts of people have recognised the importance of this book. Here's what General 'Too Tall' Jennings had to say:

'The great strength of this book is that it not only becomes a sort of "guide, philosopher and friend" to keep beside you through the day because of all its brilliant ideas, but you also find yourself coming up with new ones of your own which work even better!'

But he had to say that, because we told him that if he didn't we'd thump him.

Lord Arthur Platt of Finsbury Park said this:

'Look guys, you're bluffing ... you'd never ... aargh ... I would never recommend a book just because ... aargh... I'd been threat- aargh ... AAARGH ... SELDOM IS ONE LUCKY ENOUGH TO COME ACROSS SUCH A USEFUL ... AARGH ... *VITAL* WONDERFUL BOOK. Can you stop now?'

You see boring adults hate this book because it means that you will be able to get away with things that they always got punished for. It's so carefully put together and so full of ideas for fooling them, they can't stand it. In fact we've heard of teachers and other adults buying up all the copies of this book so that their children can't get hold of them.

So very well done on getting hold of a copy. Keep it safe. Read it only when no one else is about. If it falls into the wrong hands, it could be used against you.

If you do read any of it and you then see an adult, don't forget to give it to the adult straight away saying that you are very sorry –

BANG! BANG!

Sorry about that; somehow, an adult infiltrated the book and started writing bits. See how clever they are? And how determined to stop this book?

Well, we've sorted that adult out. As you may have guessed from the 'BANGS!'
a little earlier and the crumpled body on the floor – it's nasty but it's a jungle out here – we crept up behind the adult and shouted BANG!

Anyway, now it's your turn to help yourself. And live a little! We wish you the best of luck and we leave you with the words of Norman Toaser MP:

'Adults can be fooled, with just a little planning, a certain amount of good luck and an occasional tea bag*.'

*Not altogether sure what he meant by this.

part one
Starting the Day

GETTING UP

ADULTS DON'T REALISE THAT GETTING UP IS BAD FOR YOU.

This is a shame as it means they rush around waking everybody up and forcing them out of bed and down to breakfast.

It is easy to show by statistics that this is unsafe: World War I. The Great Fire Of London. The American Civil War. The so called 'Six Day War' in the Middle East. *How many of these would have happened if the people involved had not got out of bed? NONE! That's how many.* **HA!**

There are stories which show this to be true. For example, there is the parable of:

The Three Men In An Accident Prone Village

The first man got up very early and set off for work. Because it was still dark, he fell down a manhole. The second man got up *quite* early, and he too set off for work. He died in mysterious circumstances, which the police are still investigating. The third man got up at a reasonable time, but he got hit by a bus.

Hmm. Perhaps the meaning of that story is a little . . . er . . . obscure. Ah, we've got another parable. It is:

The Parable Of The One Man Who Got Up Early And Exploded.

Yes, well, I don't think we really need to bother with that one.

So, anyway, getting up is something to avoid. But hiding under the covers and making a noise which implies you are not there is no good at all. However tempting it may be to try this, you must remember that it is

completely pointless.

Many people have tried it as a tactic for avoiding the day, including Margaret Thatcher and, some time ago, General Custer. It is also a well-recorded historical fact that on the day of his execution, Charles II pretended to be still asleep under the covers. However, the Chief Executioner did not believe him.

That is why it is crucial to have some proper ways of avoiding getting up.

HERE THEY COME

1 THE DREAM SCHEME

1   Listen to the early morning news on a radio in your bedroom.

2   Memorise three of the news items.

3   When you go down to breakfast say that you had a dream that a number of things would happen today.

4   First, recite the news items you've learnt, then add:

'and I also dreamt that for some unspecified reason it would be very dangerous for me to go into school today.'

HOLD THE MIDDLE PAGE 2

At breakfast, read the local paper, then suddenly tear a piece out of it. Hide it and pretend you've torn out the item below:

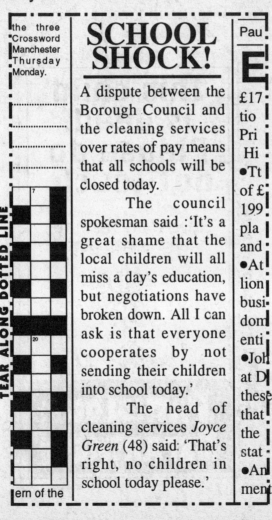

the three
Crossword
Manchester
Thursday
Monday.

TEAR ALONG DOTTED LINE

SCHOOL SHOCK!

A dispute between the Borough Council and the cleaning services over rates of pay means that all schools will be closed today.

The council spokesman said : 'It's a great shame that the local children will all miss a day's education, but negotiations have broken down. All I can ask is that everyone cooperates by not sending their children into school today.'

The head of cleaning services *Joyce Green* (48) said: 'That's right, no children in school today please.'

ern of the

Pau
E
£17
tio
Pri
Hi
•Tt
of £
199
pla
and
•At
lion
busi
dom
enti
•Jol
at D
these
that
the
stat
•An
ment

3 DEAD IN THE MIDDLE OF THE ROOM

To give yourself a bit of an extra lie-in, cut this out and put it over your big toe.

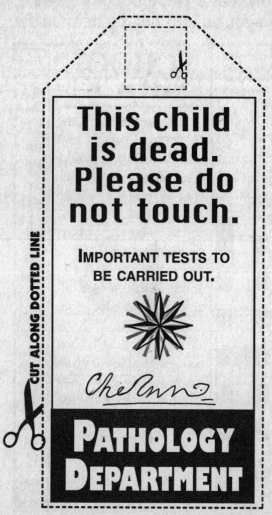

CUT ALONG DOTTED LINE

This child is dead. Please do not touch.

IMPORTANT TESTS TO BE CARRIED OUT.

PATHOLOGY DEPARTMENT

CLOCK THIS 4

To give yourself an extra hour in bed, put all the clocks in the house back by one hour.

The wrist watches of your family may be rather more tricky, but ask to borrow them the previous night on the grounds that you need to draw them for homework.

5 TAKE NOTICE

Cut out this notice and sign your name at the bottom. Then pin it to the door of your room.

CUT ALONG DOTTED LINE

I've gone to school early to look up what dis ease my new pet mice have got.

They look like this

i've shut them in my room, so they won't be in any

danger, as long as you don't open the door.

LOVE

16

TO THE LETTER 6

Cut this letter out and leave it on your doormat, as if it's just been posted through the letterbox

✂ **CUT ALONG DOTTED LINE**

𝕺𝕱𝕱𝕴𝕮𝕴𝕬𝕷 𝕾𝕮𝕳𝕺𝕺𝕷 𝕻𝕬𝕻𝕰𝕽

(Only to be used for important letters)

Dear Parent

Because everyone at school has been working so hard recently, I've decided to give the whole school a day off.

Yours sincerely,

[signature]

(Head Teacher)

7 THE NEWS PLOY

You will need:
one radio cassette recorder

1 Get up at 6.00 a.m., switch on your radio, and copy down the radio news bulletin.

2 Put in a blank cassette and set the machine to record.

3 Read the news bulletin into the tape recorder, but insert the following item:
'A local school was flooded today. The (*say your school's name here*) school is three feet under water and staff say there is no chance of there being any lessons. Pupils are asked to stay away completely.'

4 At breakfast say: 'I wonder what's on the radio?' and turn the tape on.

IN-CAR ENTERTAINMENT

To avoid setting off from the house, simply unhinge the coddler alternating flange on the family car.

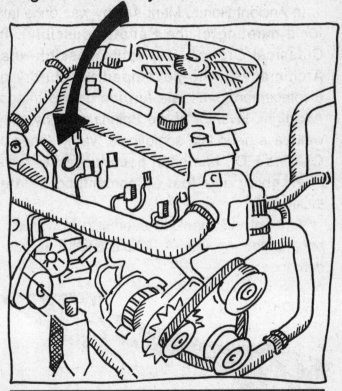

N.B. It is only suggested you try this one if you are a qualified mechanic and have passed a reasonably wide variety of car mechanic exams and have also answered car mechanic questions correctly when you've been stopped in the street by plain clothes undercover car mechanic examiners.

GETTING TO SCHOOL

THE CONCEPT OF BEING 'LATE' FOR SOMETHING IS a common feature of all major civilisations in the history of the world.

In Ancient Rome, Mark Antony was once late for a meeting of the Senate (possibly). In Classical Greece, it is quite possible that Archimedes, who developed the theory of displacement, was late for one or two things. Arkwright, inventor of the Spinning Jenny, may well have been late sometimes. Vinny Jones of Chelsea F.C., has often been judged to have been guilty of a foul by committing a 'late' tackle.*

And yet still mankind seems to frown upon people who are late. A '**reason**' is often demanded.

* By way of contrast, there is a tribe living in the South American rain forest which has no concept of time. They are therefore never late, and never early, and everyone is very relaxed. However, they do find it difficult to have boiled eggs the way they like them and they regularly miss their favourite television programmes.

Example: You are late for school. Should you:

(a) explain that, in a historical context, your lateness is neither surprising nor necessarily impolite, but a link with some of the highest points of human evolution?

(b) lie?

These days it is no longer enough merely to say 'The bus was late,' 'The cat was ill on my hair,' or 'I fell over.'

Here are some excuses you can try

Dear School,   Mrs Rochester

How nice it is to come across a really well brought up child!

I am an elderly lady and I slipped and fell over on a patch of wet pavement. I could have fractured the head of my left femur, but fortunately it was just a soft tissue injury, and the prospects of full mobilisation in the short term are good.

Anyway, up came this child and helped me in every way possible, calling an ambulance, cordoning off the area and taking photographs for my possible legal action against the council. It really was tremendous.

Sorry that this will have meant that my little helper was a bit late!

Love

Mrs Rochester.

FANTASTIC 2

Insert your teacher's name in the note below and say that the reason you are late is because you spotted your teacher's favourite TV actor in the street and had to chase them for ages for their autograph.

✂ **CUT ALONG DOTTED LINE**

To

I hear you're a fan of the show. Please keep watching as keeping you entertained is what we're all there for! With love from me and all the cast,

P.S. This child is a credit to you

23

3 TWO EXCUSES TO AVOID

When you are accused of being late, you *can* say either:

(a) 'I am in fact 23 hours early for tomorrow.'

OR

(b) 'Such concentration on the theory of space-time continuum is an unnecessarily narrow-minded approach to life.'

But you should not, unless your teacher is totally deaf and unable to lip read, or you were going to leave the school anyway.

CERTIFICATE 4

Fill in this document with your name, cut it out and give it to your Head Teacher to sign.

✂ **CUT ALONG DOTTED LINE**

TO THE
HEAD TEACHER

This is to certify that

....

has entered the Sponsored
Getting to School Late Competition.

The later he/she gets to school, the more money is raised for the *Rain Forests in Brazil*, the *Royal National Life Boat Institute*, and the *Bat Colony in the Isle of Skye*, even though this may all be a bit surprising. Please fill in and detach the form below and return it to the above address.

Please verify that the holder was late:
I,..
a Head Teacher, do solemnly swear that this child was ....minutes late.

5 TYRE PUNCTURE 1

You will need:
one bicycle inner tube

All you need to do is to say that you had a puncture – no one will disbelieve you if you have the inner tube with you.

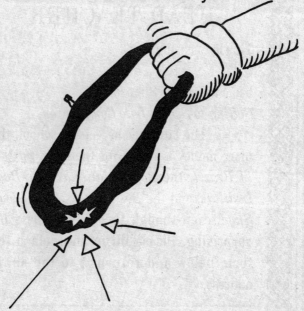

For advanced students only:

Add that you got the puncture when skidding to avoid a small child who ran out into the road.

26

TYRE PUNCTURE 2 6

You will need:
a small quantity of oil

Explain that you had to help change the wheel on an ambulance which was on a mercy dash.

If no one believes you, say: 'I didn't expect to be believed, but do you mind if I wash this oil off my hands?'

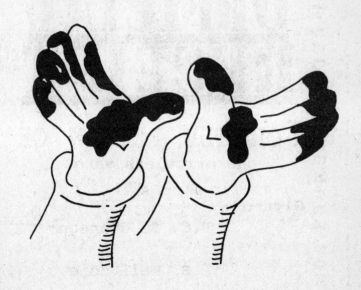

7 LOCAL HERO

Say that you recognised a vase on the rubbish dump as a priceless oriental Ming recently shown on *Crimewatch*, and that you had to hand it in to the police.

✂ **CUT ALONG DOTTED LINE**

OFFICIAL RECEIPT NUMBER 999

POLICE OFFICIAL RECEIPT

FOR THE RETURN OF
one priceless vase

Signed *P.C. S. Johnson*
P.C. S. Johnson

P.S. Well done.

SOLIDARITY 8

Show the teacher this card, having filled in your details.

✂ **CUT ALONG DOTTED LINE**

SCHOOL CHILDREN'S UNION CARD

This child is a fully paid up union member

FOLD ALONG DOTTED LINE

PASSPORT PHOTOGRAPH

Child's Name:
_____

Date _____
Age _____

School _____

Announce that you are on a go-slow in support of higher rates of pay for teachers.

9 DENTIST'S LETTER

Simply fill in your name and hand to your teacher. ✂ **CUT ALONG DOTTED LINE**

RENT~A~DENTIST

✝ ✝ ✝ ✝ ✝ ✝ ✝ ✝ ✝ ✝ ✝ ✝

Dear ....

This is to confirm your appointment for 8:45 today. We've got all the tools ready, together with the mouthwash and the big black chair and the bright lights.

Looking forward to getting your gnashers into tip-top condition!

Yours

[signature]

Dentist

✝ ✝ ✝ ✝ ✝ ✝ ✝ ✝ ✝ ✝ ✝ ✝

DÉJA VU 10

Explain that someone unhinged the coddler alternating flange from your car's engine (see page 19). Show them this diagram to explain.

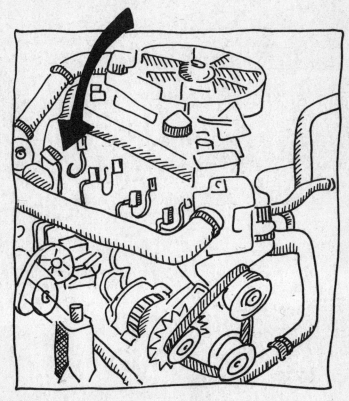

Remember not to have the coddler alternating flange and attached plug leads on you at this moment.

part two

Homework Excuses

HOMEWORK

FORGETTING TO DO YOUR HOMEWORK IS perfectly reasonable when there are so many more interesting and useful things to occupy your time, but teachers can become very one-track-minded and suspicious about this. So we have endeavoured to come up with a number of water-tight excuses.

We must however sound a note of caution: each excuse can only be used on the same teacher once. And some teachers now carry a list of excuses taped to the inside of the register so they can match up excuses to ones that have been used before.

There is also a teacher's handbook recently translated from the German entitled *Tips For Teachers*.* Inside, among other things, is a section entitled 'Spotting Homework Excuses A Mile Off', which will render many homework excuses useless. How can you tell if your teacher is using this book? Well, it also has all kinds of suggested remarks for teachers to make, such as:

---

* At the present time we are trying to sneak a few pages of our own into the revised version of Tips For Teachers. These pages come to the unlikely conclusion that teachers should wear a suit of armour and eat plenty of cheese. So if your teacher shows signs of doing either of these things (though not necessarily in that order), you will know that we have been successful.

'This class is so much noisier than last year's.'

'That's neither clever nor funny.'

'It's your own time you're wasting.'

'I'm really disappointed with you.'

So if your teacher starts using these phrases,

BEWARE.

But we've tried very hard to keep ahead of the teachers and the excuses here are very nearly guaranteed to get you out of all kinds of sticky situations. For example, our publishers stipulated that this book should have 160 pages, but we used some of the excuses at the right time because we had only written 144 and they believed us! It just shows you how successful excuses can be. If they work on a multi-million pound book publishers like Knight Books (who have no end of clever people), think how easily they should be able to fool your teacher.

So, no longer will it be 'I forgot sir/miss,' 'My dog ate it,' 'I left it on the bus,' or 'The wind blew it away.' Read on and commit these excuses to memory, so that you have them at your fingertips at the moment of emergency. (See also Part 6 *Homework*, page 89.)

1

WRONG HOMEWORK

Say you did the wrong homework by mistake. Cut out the page of maths equations below to use as proof.

✂ CUT ALONG DOTTED LINE

$$9y + 3 = 30$$

$$9y = 30 - 3$$

$$9y = 27$$

$$y = 27/9$$

$$y = 3$$

WORD PLAY 2

Say you decided to do your homework on the word processor at home so that it would be really neat. However the printer went wrong:

✂ **CUT ALONG DOTTED LINE**

–•¶•§   ¢∞#≈ ™¥∂
¥©øu©øuioj
–ºª(*(^UKHJ_)P–•
¶•§   ¢∞#≈™¥∂   ¥
©øuio   j–ºª(*(^
UKHJ_)P
–•¶•§   ¢∞#≈™¥∂
¥   ©øuio
j – º ª (* (^ &
UKHJ_)P–•¶•§¢∞
#≈™¥∂ ¥ © øuij
_ºª   (*(^
&UKHJ_)P
¶•§   ¢∞#≈™¥∂   ¥
©øuio   j–ºª(*(^
UKHJ_)P–•¶•§¥∂

3 BURNING POINT

Hand in this page which you say you managed to rescue when your elder brother or a bully tried to burn your work:

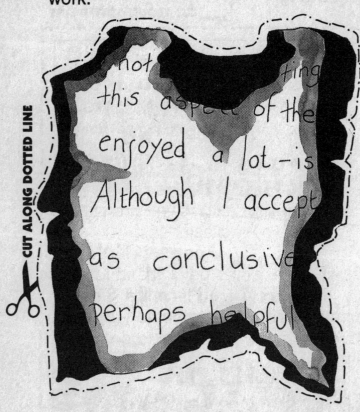

CUT ALONG DOTTED LINE

...not ...ting
this aspect of the
enjoyed a lot — is
Although I accept

as conclusive

perhaps helpful

SPRAINED ARM 4

1 Get a large square piece of cloth, and follow the diagrams on the following page which show you how to fold it into a sling.

2 Put your writing arm in the sling and say you have sprained it. This should not only get you off homework but also help you avoid having to do any work at all for a couple of days.

Remember to say you have just sprained rather than broken it, as you are unlikely to be able to get a plaster cast.

However, if you can mix up some plaster of Paris and get a friend to put it on your arm, you'll miss out on homework for a few months – but you may have some explaining to do to your parents.

TURN PAGE FOR DIAGRAMS →

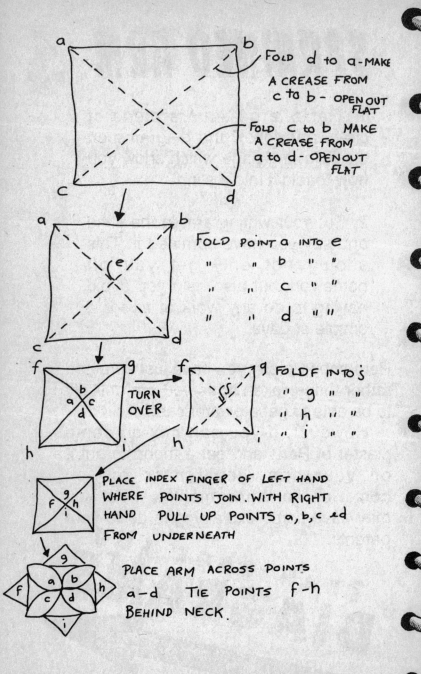

FOLD d to a – MAKE A CREASE FROM c to b – OPEN OUT FLAT

FOLD c to b MAKE A CREASE FROM a to d – OPEN OUT FLAT

FOLD POINT a INTO e
" " b " "
" " c " "
" " d " "

TURN OVER

FOLD F INTO s
" g " "
" h " "
" i " "

PLACE INDEX FINGER OF LEFT HAND WHERE POINTS JOIN. WITH RIGHT HAND PULL UP POINTS a, b, c & d FROM UNDERNEATH

PLACE ARM ACROSS POINTS a–d TIE POINTS f–h BEHIND NECK.

SICK NOTE 1 5

Cut out and hand to your teacher.

✂ **CUT ALONG DOTTED LINE**

> Dear Teacher,
>
> My child, is very ill with small pox, cholera, measles and a stubbed toe. That is why there will be no homework from him/her* this morning. Honest.
>
> Yours
> his/her* Mum

*delete as appropriate.

SICK NOTE 2

Cut out and hand to your teacher.

CUT ALONG DOTTED LINE

DOCTOR'S PAPER

Dear Teacher,

This child is very ill. All will be well, however, if the subject of homework is never mentioned. If it is, my patient will become very violent with guns, knives and things.

Particularly towards teachers.

Yours sincerely

Psychiatrist

RAINED ON ESSAY 7

On a rainy day, this page of rained on homework could be invaluable.

✂ **CUT ALONG DOTTED LINE**

but ... the various different versions are compared, some ... differences can be notice... for instance, while the first ... says that there were over one thousand, the second estimates the number at several hundred, and the third does not refer to the number at all. This may or ... relevant, but it does cast doubt on the reliability

8 *TEACHER GUIDE*

If you come across certain types of teacher, there are some extra responses possible when asked for homework.

(a) The Timid Teacher

You can say: 'I had more important things to do.'

(b) The Trendy Teacher

You can say: 'Do you think students should be punished for not doing their homework? Isn't it more important for the teacher to encourage a better pupil/teacher relationship based on trust and goodwill?'

(c) The Student Teacher

You do not have to do any work for this kind of teacher, particularly if you make a bargain with him or her to look as though you *are* working when the supervisor comes in to watch how he or she is getting on.

(d) The Strict Teacher

Put your arm in a sling (see page 39) and say: 'I'm sorry I haven't done my homework. I know how much you hate people who don't do their homework, so I've already punished myself by spraining my own arm.'

part
three
Lessons

PAYING ATTENTION

Sadly, even on a good day, teachers can be unreasonable. Let's say you've got up all by yourself, had breakfast, left the comfort of your own home, got to school on time, handed in your homework and sat down without setting fire to the furniture.

THEY STILL WANT MORE.

If you can believe it, they actually want you to pay attention. This is of course . . . er . . . where were we? . . . Oh yes, this is something which should not be expected of you all the time.

The mind should be a free spirit, not hemmed in, restrained, chained up, locked in, told to stay in a certain place for a bit, or handcuffed to a radiator for five years. Strictly speaking, it shouldn't even be told to go to its room early because of a harmless little remark made in a spirit of fun which seems to have been misunderstood.

Would Thomas Edison have discovered the secret of electric light if he'd concentrated on the irregular verb 'aller' (to go)?

Would Graham Taylor have rediscovered the strength of Gary Mabbut's defensive awareness if he'd been forced to do equations whilst bound and gagged in a dark room?

NO.

Would Alexander Fleming have discovered penicillin if he had been told to find and chart the North-West passage?

Um . . . I don't really understand these questions any more. So,

it is a good thing that the mind wanders since you are likely to become a more imaginative and creative person.

However, teachers can find this concept hard to understand. Having some ready-made answers available means you needn't worry about being asked a question when you are not listening or to which you don't know the answer. You can therefore let your mind wander as freely as you like (possibly inventing the air car*).

* Remember that with an air car the aerodynamics may have less effect on the efficiency than the power/weight ratio.

1 ENGLISH

Say: 'Oh, I'm sorry, I was composing a poem,' and try to pull a face like this one.

If pressed, see the emergency poem on the following page.

THE EMERGENCY POEM

Just insert your own name in the
following:

✂ **CUT ALONG DOTTED LINE**

My name is _____ ,
It's my name all day long,
People say, 'Hey _____ ,
Sing a happy song.'

So I say: 'Of all the things
        that I like best,
My favourite food is kippers.
I've put one in Dad's vest,
And several in his slippers.'

People say, 'You're naughty,
        _____,'
They say it all the time.
They say, 'You couldn't be a
        worse child,_____,'
But I'll use live fish next
        time.

HISTORY

Say: 'I was just thinking of how this relates to the development of the Spinning Jenny in 1764. Can you see the connection sir/miss?'

Try and pull a face like this one:

GEOGRAPHY 3

Say: 'I was wondering whether this would change when the climate gets warmer. If there was a change, how would we measure it?'

Try and pull a face like this one:

4 SCIENCE

Say: 'I was just thinking. Let's assume an arrow is fired at someone's head a distance of *y* away.

'To begin with, it must travel half of that distance leaving the other half still untravelled. So it has travelled half of *y* and still has half of *y* to go.

'Of the remaining distance, it must first travel the first half of it, leaving the second half untravelled.

'Then of that remaining distance it must travel the first half, leaving the second half untravelled.

'And so it will continue always travelling the first half of the remaining distance but leaving the second half untravelled.

'Does this mean that the arrow will never reach the head, and therefore King Harold died of shock?'

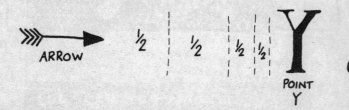

ARROW   ½   ½   ½ ½   Y

POINT Y

You will need:
one live rat

1 Keep the rat well hidden.

2 When asked a question, say, 'Sorry, I was wondering what species this rat is.'

6 DRAMA

Say: 'I was thinking about the part. Frankly, you've rather spoilt my concentration. Now I will do some interpretative dance.'

For the interpretative dance, you can do the sort of thing shown below until it's been forgotten that you've been asked a question.

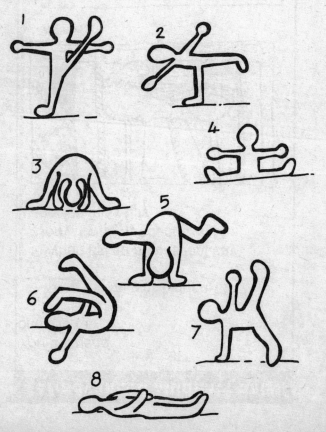

RELIGIOUS STUDIES 7

Say: 'Oh teacher, I was listening to the sound of one hand clapping.'

8 ART

In art, you are more likely to be asked why you are making so much noise. Usually the conversation goes like this:

TEACHER (rather loudly): 'What did I just say?'

PUPIL: '"Don't make so much noise", sir/miss.'

TEACHER: 'So why are you making all that row?'

At this point, saying 'Don't know sir/miss,' is usually enough, but if this is wearing thin after seven or eight uses, have this picture in reserve, and say: 'We were just arguing about who was the dominant influence on this – Rembrandt or Van Haals?'

ALL PURPOSE 1 9

You will need:
a piece of metal

Carry this with you at all times.
　　When asked a difficult question, pretend to take it out of your mouth and say: 'I'm sorry, but I'm afraid one of my fillings has just come out,' and show the teacher the piece of metal.

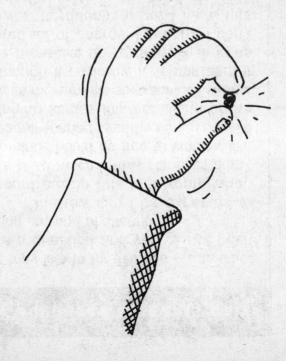

For advanced students only:

You may like to try this one if a teacher asks a question and you've not been paying any sort of attention.

'Oh, how can I be expected to concentrate on this little room when there is so much in this planet of ours? The mind should be free to wander like a seagull soaring over the surf, a gazelle springing across the wasteland of the wild, its movements so graceful it seems as though it could fly, it seems as if it were more like poetry than flesh in its blurred jet of energy. I'm sorry I can't answer the question, but I have this wonderful vision in my head, a vision that maybe, one day, all mankind's spirits will be as free as that bird and that gazelle, gliding in the warm tropical air of mutual respect and true understanding.'

IMPORTANT NOTE: This one doesn't work all that often, but if you get the right teacher, you probably won't have to do any work for a month.

TESTING TIMES

If you have a lesson coming up with a test for which you have not prepared, you may well want to cut out and use the notice below. Hopefully, this will delay the lesson sufficiently while the caretaker is called etc., so that there will be no time for the test.

✂ ━ **CUT ALONG DOTTED LINE**

N O T I C E
TO ANYONE
INTENDING TO USE
THIS CLASSROOM

DANGER!
KEEP OUT

THIS CLASSROOM IS TOTALLY UNSAFE FOR A NUMBER OF REASONS MAINLY RELATING TO THE FOUNDATIONS ETC.

part four

Break

BREAK

İT IS A BIOLOGICAL FACT THAT EVERYONE NEEDS A
break during the day.

As David Attenborough said in his
authoritative BBC documentary *Life On Earth*
and in his major television series *The Trials of
Life*, 'Oh, I really could do with a break.'

Although, in fact, this was cut out of the final
versions of both series.

He also said, 'I could do with some nice
Swiss cheese,' but at this point we asked him
to keep the noise down, because, frankly, he
was becoming a bit of a pain.

Anyway, so, the point is, right, that everyone
needs a break. And – this is very important –
you should never be fooled by the so-called
adults into thinking that they don't have breaks.

Why do you think you are never allowed into
the staff room? It's because nearly all schools
are designed with a secret underground playing
area which leads off from the staff room itself.

We decided to investigate.

Acting on a tip-off from a source close to the
HM, reasonably close to the LM and miles
away from the PQ, we paid £40,000 for false
documents and teacher disguises (piles of
exercise books, petri dishes, unfashionable

clothes, tired looks, and bitter words and phrases such as 'low morale', 'unsatisfactory pay and conditions' and 'I'm a teacher, you know').We then went undercover to see one of these teachers' playgrounds in operation.

Sadly, the scene that greeted us was all too predictable: many of the teachers were playing football or skipping; some were bullying the Art Master in the corner by tying his shoe laces together, nicking his packed lunch, and tickling him quite hard; the rest were just running around, screaming (see Artist's Impression No 4 [sorry about Artist's Impressions Nos 1, 2 and 3 – the artist got rather the wrong end of the stick]).

So don't feel teachers are doing you a favour by giving you a break.

It's your right.

You must protect it and extend it whenever possible.

68

EXTRA TIME

If you'd like a slightly longer break than usual, hand this to the teacher on break duty.

✂ **CUT ALONG DOTTED LINE**

School Memo

From: The Head Teacher

To: The Teacher Supervising Break

Please allow the children an extra ten minutes' break today. It's my birthday and I'm feeling generous.

Remind me to give you some tea and buns to celebrate, after school.

I hope you are well. I am.

Head Teacher

2 BREAK DUTY

As a rather more extreme alternative, you might try giving this to the teacher on break duty.

CUT ALONG DOTTED LINE

give The kids an Extra ten minutes Break or Else

AVOIDING BULLIES

If you get challenged to a fight, say: 'Certainly, but I am obliged to show you this first.'

✂ **CUT ALONG DOTTED LINE**

KARATE CERTIFICATE

This certificate has been awarded to

_____

Date_____/_____/_____

He/she is licensed to really hurt other people.
(No kidding.)

4 BREAKAGE

If your ball goes through a window, grab as many balls with other people's names on as you can, and throw those through the window as well.

This will make it difficult to prove who did the damage.

FIGHTING 5

(a) If you are caught fighting with an enemy, say: 'He/she said you weren't a very good teacher.'

(b) If you are caught fighting with a friend, say: 'We were trying to act out that scene in last night's film – did it look realistic?'

NOTE: *Why you might be fighting with a friend is not clear, but it's best to be prepared for every eventuality.*

part
five
Games

GAMES

If it was proved that an activity outside the classroom tired people out, carried with it the risk of injury, forced people to face cold and wet weather in inadequate clothing, and involved unproductive use of time and money, you might have thought that a school would ban it. In fact, you might have thought that they would call in the police, round up the ringleaders and put them in prison.

INSTEAD, GAMES ARE COMPULSORY.

It could be asked why they're called games at all. It's not as if you get to play Cluedo, Ker-Plunk or Kill The President.

Of course, some people say that the Battle of Waterloo was won on the playing fields of Eton, but that just goes to show how stupid they are. Eton is near Windsor, whereas Waterloo is a railway station in south London.

Other people say:

'Sport is at its finest when it combines the body, mind, spirit and soul - as in table tennis,'

or

'Table tennis is the language of kings.'

And as some people say back to that,

'Ping, pong, bop, bib, bippity, bipperty, BAP – whaaaa! Love - one.'

Which all goes to show how boring you can become if you allow games to become your life.*

With the help of the following pages, you can now control what psychologists call

'The Games Situation'.

*There is a rumour that the Austro-Hungarian Revolution was sparked off by an unfortunate edge ball after a high top spin lob by Leopold of Austria.

1 INJURY

To get off games cut out the note below and hand it to your games teacher.

✂ **CUT ALONG DOTTED LINE**

The Beveridge Health Centre, Church Street

To Whom It May Concern

This child has a recurrent hamstring problem, or maybe it's a groin strain. Either way they have failed a late fitness test carried out this morning, and will be sidelined for the foreseeable future.

'Och, I'm terribly disappointed,' said the young player after my examination this morning, 'but the Doc says I've just got to be patient and build up slowly.'

Signed

DR ~~(signature)~~

(A Doctor)

I am another Doctor who happened to be in the neighbourhood and I fully agree with all of the above.

Signed

DR ~~(signature)~~.

(Another Doctor)

EXHAUSTION 2

Fill in yesterday's date below the competitor number, cut out the whole thing and pin it on your vest. Then say you are exhausted because you ran a marathon the night before in Yeovil for charity. Point to the number as proof.

CUT ALONG DOTTED LINE

YEOVIL
Marathon

COMPETITOR NUMBER

7469

Date

3 AVOIDING P.E. 1

Say: 'Excuse me, I've just cross-referenced my bio-rhythms with my pasta-loading schedule and the flow-chart for my stamina work-out, and today is a rest day.'

Use the chart below if there is a credibility problem.

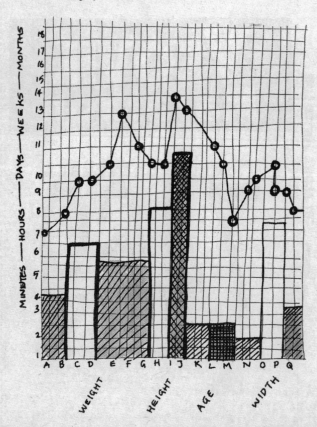

AVOIDING P.E. 2

Fill in convenient dates in this letter and present it to your teacher.

✂ **CUT ALONG DOTTED LINE**

BRITISH YOUTH ATHLETICS ASSOCIATION GRIMSBY

Dear Teacher,
        We have a big athletics meeting on

. . . .

Please ensure this pupil is thoroughly rested before it.

I know that the pupil will be wanting to do lots of exercise, but please insist that they take no part in games and remain fresh.

        Yours

Fill in, cut out and hand to the appropriate teacher.

✂ **CUT ALONG DOTTED LINE**

SCHOOL SPORTS FEDERATION
Head Office: Pall Mall, London

This is to certify that ....
has passed the
Nationally Approved Standard for

....

and therefore does not need to do the test again.

Signed _(signature)_
(Director)

Signed _(signature)_
(Treasurer)

Signed _(signature)_
(Secretary)

Signed _(signature)_
(Person In Charge Of Tests)

If you are unable to get out of playing games, it is important to assess your teacher correctly before the lesson starts. They fall into one of two categories.

(a) The Keen Games Teacher

This type is dangerously keen and fit. Get on his good side by asking about the selection of any current international team.

This type is very pleased if you just try hard, so you'll be OK if you can just splash water on yourself every ten minutes to make it look like you're sweating.

83

(b) The Unkeen Games Teacher

This one won't notice if you are there or not.

If you do turn up, you will probably be able to persuade them that the International Federation of (whatever sport you're playing) has recently changed the rules to allow for half of you to sit down and an early finish.

FORGOTTEN P.E. KIT 7

If you've forgotten your kit and don't want your teacher to notice, one of the following ruses may work.

(a) By Design

Cut out these designer labels and stick them to your ordinary clothes. Then pretend they are the latest style in fashion sports wear.

CUT ALONG DOTTED LINE

BRAVANTI
Sports wear

'For All Athletes'
(Especially brilliant ones)

Made In Italy

CUT ALONG DOTTED LINE

BRAVANTI
Sports wear

'For All Athletes'
(Especially brilliant ones)

Made In Italy

(b)Guinea Pig

Cut out this note and hand it to your games teacher.

CUT ALONG DOTTED LINE

A.A.A.

This pupil is participating in the Amateur Athletics Association and British Sports Council research scheme for this year.

The object is to see if people perform better in games kit or in ordinary clothes. Today, this pupil should wear ordinary clothes

Please co-operate in every way possible.

Thank you.

(c)Modulated

Announce that you are doing Module F.2. of the new National Curriculum

National Curriculum

New revised edition

GAMES AND SPORTS

Includes:

Module F.1.
     Games in games kit

Module F.2.
     Games **not** in games kit

Handy Things To Shout In Any Sport When You want To Stand Still For A Bit

Always remember to put your hand in the air and turn to the teacher *as* you say them.

'Offside!'

'Foul!'

'Ow!' (Clutch your hamstring when using this one. **More advanced students** can try pulling up on the run with a kind of hopping motion to make it look even more authentic.)

'Referee!'

'Ours!'

'Every time – they do that every time!'

'Off the ball incident!'(See if you can spin though the air for this one.)

'Come on, think about it – think about *space*, team.'

'Watch the options everyone.'

'Come on, we've got to turn up to this game, otherwise we'll have a mountain to climb.'

'Bananas, 56 pence a pound.' (If asked about this, pretend you were trying to put the other side off.)

'Let's try a wide 1-2.'

For advanced students only:

'Melt down expected. Danger Will Robinson! Scotty, give me everything you've got. I can't hold her Captain, she's breaking up.'

88

part six

six

Homework

AVOIDING HOMEWORK

AS THE EARTH COOLED AT THE DAWN OF TIME IT formed three things: the land, the sea and homework.* Up until then, there had been almost nothing to learn about, but suddenly there was stacks – geography, physics, biology, chemistry and lots more (although it was another 4 million years before English Literature raised its ugly head and said 'This is your homework for tonight!').

There is a theory that certain prominent people throughout history have sought to create homework just for the sake of it.

For example, if Arkwright had not invented the Spinning Jenny in 1764 we wouldn't have to learn about it for homework. Similarly, if Nelson had not fought the battle of Trafalgar in 1805, that would have been one less piece of homework for everyone, and an evening off.

Some people conclude from this that Nelson was just a grumpy old man who wanted to keep people in. However there is evidence which suggests that this piece of homework was not Nelson's fault, because the battle was

* 'Rubbish!' Sir David Attenborough

forced on him by King Louis the Killjoy of France, and that Nelson avoided fighting battles at Dogger, Bank, Fortes, Whitley Bay and the sands at Blackpool, because he realised that this would mean a whole week of staying in for extra homework.

Of course, homework can sometimes be worthwhile. It can be quite fun to see the pathetic way a teacher's face will light up when you actually bother to hand something in. Also, if you are being taught by Commander 'Mad Dog' Blackwoody of the 9th/12th Marines, having homework available will prevent you being keel-hauled through the school pond.

BUT JUST BECAUSE YOU'VE GOT TO GET YOUR HOMEWORK DONE DOESN'T MEAN *YOU* HAVE TO DO IT.

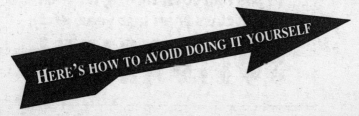

HERE'S HOW TO AVOID DOING IT YOURSELF

1 STRIKE

During the day at school, cut out this page and leave it on your teacher's desk or slip it under the staff room door during break.

CUT ALONG DOTTED LINE

N.U.T.

(National Union of Teachers)

Teachers' Strike

URGENT NEWS

All teachers are requested to go on an emergency 'Not Setting Any Homework Strike' today. This urgent action is in support of all the usual things (you know – low pay, low morale, staff shortages, having to have 1970s haircuts, having a much noisier class than last year, etc.).

SOLIDARITY!

COUPONS

2

Cut out these coupons and give them to your teacher instead of homework.

✂ CUT ALONG DOTTED LINE

HISTORY HOMEWORK

To the pupil: Cut out and hand in this coupon in place of one (1) piece of History homework.

To the teacher: This coupon may only be accepted in place of History homework. Send this coupon to the Department of Education who will refund you one (1) piece of relevant homework.

✂ CUT ALONG DOTTED LINE

MATHS HOMEWORK

To the pupil: Cut out and hand in this coupon in place of one (1) piece of Maths homework.

To the teacher: This coupon may only be accepted in place of Maths homework. Send this coupon to the Department of Education who will refund you one (1) piece of Maths homework.

3 GETTING OTHERS TO DO YOUR HOMEWORK

If the homework really has to be done, then for once your parents may come in useful.

YOUR MOTHER

(a) Temptation
'I'd love to tell you the rumour about Mrs (neighbour's name), but I've got to do my homework.'

(b) Sympathy
'Mum, you helping me with my homework would help to take my mind off the fact that I haven't got my own dog.'

(c) Blackmail
'Mum, I've got this tape of you and Dad arguing and (friend's name) wants me to go round to their house and play it, but I said I couldn't go as you'd be helping me with my homework.'

(d) Bringing Out the Best in Her
'Everyone is always saying that Mrs (friend's mother's name) is wonderful. Do you know

she helps her children with their homework every night? They're always saying what a great mother she is.'

YOUR FATHER

(a) Challenge His generation
'Homework is far harder now than it was when you were at school – I mean, you probably couldn't answer these questions.'

(b) Appeal to His Better Nature
'Dad, I'm doing a sponsored charity quiz. You agree to pay some money for every question you don't know. So if you get them all right, you won't have to pay any money.'

(c) Challenge His Pride
'Dad, I've bet (friend's name) that you know more than his dad and we've decided to settle it with a general knowledge competition.'

(d) Tickle His Sense of Fun
'Dad, can we play game shows? I'll be quiz master.'

4 TEN SECOND HOMEWORK

If you can't get someone else to do your homework, then study these quick and easy substitute homework pages. You may not learn what your teacher meant you to learn, but at least you can truthfully say that you have studied the subject.

(a)History 1

THE END OF THE ENGLISH CIVIL WAR

Spot the difference between these two scenes:

(b)History 2

THE RIDDLE OF THE LITTLE PRINCES IN THE TOWER

You will need:
one dice

Did Richard II murder the Little Princes in the Tower?

HOW TO SOLVE THE MYSTERY:

1. Throw the dice.

2. Read the answer off this table:

     i)   'Yes he did, definitely.'

     ii)   'Yes he did, probably.'

     iii)   'Mmm, he might have.'

     iv)   'There's no real evidence.'

     v)   'He probably didn't.'

     vi)   'He didn't.'

3. If the dice is caught and eaten by a household pet say:
     'They were kidnapped by aliens.'

(c)Geography

Spot the deliberate mistake in this map:

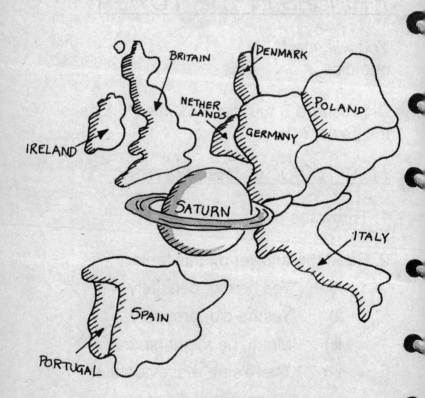

(d)Art

FORGERY

A recurrent problem in the Art World is whether or not a picture is a fake. Here is a picture which has recently been discovered to be a fake. Can you spot the little details that give it away?

(e)Nature

VITAL NATURAL RESOURCES

Of the following six items, only five are vital to mankind's survival on this planet. Can you identify which they are?

1 RAINFORESTS	2 CLEAN AIR
3 CLEAN WATER	4 ENERGY CONSERVATION
5 WASTE RECYCLING	6 MR JEREMY BEADLE

(f)Science 1

THE HISTORY OF THE LIGHTBULB

THE MAIN PROBLEM IN DESIGNING A LIGHTBULB WAS DECIDING WHAT SHAPE THE BULB SHOULD BE.

SUDDENLY, THOMAS EDISON HAD AN IDEA.

(g)Science 2

WATER

Something that tends to take water away from your body is known as a **dehydrant**, for example heat.

Something that replaces lost water after the effect of a dehydrant is known as a **rehydrant**, for example a cup of tea.

Oh, and this is a **fire hydrant**.

(h)Drama

Play the part of Jimmy or Samantha in this short play entitled *Jimmy and Samantha Live It Up*. It has been specifically designed for you to be able to say you had one of the title roles.

JIMMY AND SAMANTHA LIVE IT UP

Lights up. Kevin and Jackie are in a bare room.

Kevin: Hi, Jackie.

Jackie: Hi, Kevin.

Kevin: Been doing anything interesting recently?

Jackie: I made some yoghurt, but apart from that I've just watched television.

Kevin: Oh. Me too. Only without the television, as I spilt some yoghurt down the back. Where are Jimmy and Samantha?

Jackie: They'll be out having a good time, I expect.

Kevin: No chance of them coming round here then?

Jackie: Definitely none. I can be quite categoric about that.

Kevin: Oh, well, I'm not surprised – they're always living it up. Let's go and make some more yoghurt then.

They go. Lights dim. Abba's <u>Knowing Me, Knowing You</u> is played. Curtain.

(i)English 1

POETRY: CRITICAL RESPONSE

Read the following poem:

I, A Poet
I wonder why poets always
Write about themselves. I mean
It's not as if anyone
Is interested.
Anyway, why do some of them not rhyme
And some of them have lines of different
                                        length.
Like this.
Now I've written one; am I a poet?

Now tick which of the following critical responses you feel most accurately sums up your reaction to the poem.

A.

The poem's heavy irony is directed both at the reader and the poet. By asking for us the questions we would ask about the poem, we are simultaneously satisfied that the trivial and arbitrary nature of poetry is exposed, and yet drawn inside and agree with the thought process behind the poem. Our initial reaction that this is mockery exposing poetry wilts as we realise that the poem achieves the legitimate aim of much poetry, namely the articulation and encapsulation of a thought which we had not considered in this way. As we realise this, we are forced to concede that which we had thought the poem had disproved, namely that poetry can give us fresh insight into ourselves, whatever form it takes.

B.

An attempted defence of ametrical blank verse fails because it is forced to use what it seeks to justify, and what it uses is devoid of wit. Although the poet clearly hopes to suggest that one can poetically question poetry and thus show the resilience of the form, the answer to the rhetorical final question must still be no; one does not become a poet simply by writing lines of different lengths about oneself. Once that is established, the emperor's clothes of the structure are ripped away, and left naked is the content, a superficial and self-interested meandering.

(j)ENGLISH 2

SPELLING TEST

See if you can spell the following words.
Write your answer in the space provided.

i)   repulsive

    _____

ii)   ugly

    _____

iii) horrible

    _____

iv)   unreasonable

    _____

v)   useless

    _____

vi)   boring

    _____

vii) unwanted

    _____

viii) smelly

    _____

ix)   stupid

    _____

x)   teacher

    _____

part seven

Play

PLAY

OBVIOUSLY, THIS IS GENERALLY A GOOD BIT OF THE day. No school and you haven't got to that tense part of the evening where you start negotiating about how late you are allowed to stay up.

The thing to remember about play is that people tend to think that how you play reflects what you're going to be later in life.

For instance, Nigel Mansell used to cycle everywhere very fast.*

Terry Wogan used to go round asking pointless and stupid questions and then smiling to himself.

The chairman of British Rail used to lie in bed until 3 p.m. and then fall over because he was wearing the wrong kind of shoes.

So, think **big** at whatever you do.

* Though unfortunately, he developed a lot of problems with his tyres and gears, which his dad could never quite repair properly despite spending nearly £17 million on it, using 18 mechanics and a Black and Decker Workmate.

Don't just watch a video, *take notes and make interesting remarks after it – you could become a film critic.*

Don't just go to the shops, *buy one of them – you could be a member of the Sainsbury family (though this is unlikely if you are not already a member [although you could marry into it {but you might still have to change your name (so it's still not very likely)}]).*

Anyway, as you are unlikely to encounter problems so often during this time, the ideas here are to improve things a little bit, to nudge them along from

'really not too bad at all'

to

'absolutely brilliant'.

1 *VIDEO*

If you want to watch a rented video and would rather the rest of the family didn't know what it was, cut out the labels on this page and the next and stick them to the video and box. Attach label A to the top side of the video cassette, and label B to the spine.

On the next page is label C. You should stick this to the box.

<u>LABEL A:</u>

✂ **CUT ALONG DOTTED LINE**

Arkwright's
Spinning
✦ *Jenny* ✦
120 minutes
Narrated by Dr Jonathan Miller and Prince Charles with very detailed technical analysis and no funny bits

<u>LABEL B</u> - *For the spine*

✂ **CUT ALONG DOTTED LINE**

<u>NOT</u> SUITABLE FOR ADULTS

✂ **CUT ALONG DOTTED LINE**

Arkwright's
Spinning
Jenny:
THE
LEGEND
AND THE
⊕TRUTH⊕

Video Tutor Pack

B

JANE FONDA'S ENVIROYUM!

Jane Fonda says

'*Eating Enviroyum not only tones my figure and makes me feel healthy all the time, but it also makes me more likely to help with the gardening and other chores around the house. The main idea is to eat stacks of it.*'

A

The contents of this bag are so healthy, that I will donate 4 pence to the environment for every bag eaten.'

P r e s i d e n t

(Secretary General of the United Nations.)

If you need to keep secret the fact that you are eating sweets, simply construct this handy bag.

JOIN **A** TO **D**   JOIN **B** TO **C**
WRITING MUST BE ON OUTSIDE OF BAG

C

ISBN 0-340-27272-4

9 780340 272725

Including brussel sprouts, bits of baked potato jackets, oatcakes, cold porridge, iron and lumps of calcium!

REGISTERED AS
AN INCREDIBLY
HEALTHY THING
WITH THE
GOVERNMENT

'I would never have become a major Hollywood sensation, starring in such films as *Total Recall*, *Terminator 1*, *Twins* or *Terminator 2 – Judgement Day* without the help of Jane Fonda's *Enviroyum*.'

A. Schwarzenegger

Eat by: 7/3/2070

D

FOLD ALONG DOTTED LINE

3 FIZZY DRINKS

If fizzy drinks are rationed in your home, wrap this label around your next can.

CUT ALONG DOTTED LINE ✂

HEALTH CAN!

GUARANTEED NO SUGAR

GOOD FOR TEETH

DENTISTS RECOMMEND

DOESN'T TASTE NICE

MOST DOCTORS DRINK FOUR OR FIVE CANS A DAY (IN SECRET!)

INGREDIENTS: COD LIVER OIL, SPINACH EXTRACT, MALT, THIAMIN, B12, UNPOLISHED RICE HUSKS, WHOLE WHEAT FLOUR, SKIMMED MILK, CRAB-APPLE JELLY

TREAT

If you need your parents to give you a treat of some kind, cut out the postcard below and leave it on your own doormat.

✂ **CUT ALONG DOTTED LINE**

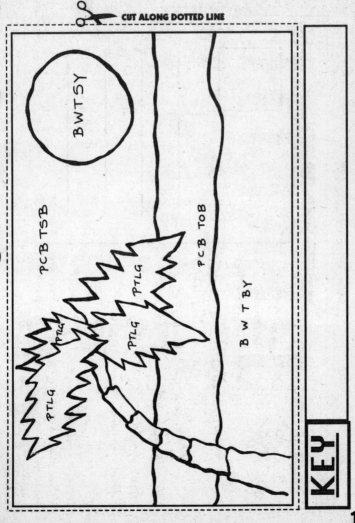

KEY

THE OTHER SIDE.

Fill in your own address here

CUT ALONG DOTTED LINE

It's great!
Peter

Sorry you couldn't
come because you
insisted on staying
home and doing chores.
Mary

I hope your parents make
it up to you like you said
they would — by taking you to
the cinema for instance. Jonathan.

We're all very sorry that you couldn't join us on this
school trip, given your consistant good behaviour
and B+ in all relevant work. This way in which
you insisted on helping your parents again - is very
impressive.
Your Teacher.

MAKING MONEY 5

1 Unhinge the coddler alternating flanges from all the cars in your road early one morning (see page 19).

2 By, say, four o'clock in the afternoon most of your neighbours will have discovered their cars have broken down, but many will not yet have got round to calling a repair man out.

3 In turn, go to each neighbour and offer to have a look at his or her car. Say you won't charge anything unless you can get it working again.

4 Clip on the coddler alternating flange.

5 £20 is an entirely reasonable rate.

6 GIVE YOURSELF A TREAT

Use the idea below if you want to go to a sports match, film or some other sporting event.

1 Leave the cards below and opposite lying around.

2 When asked about them, say you were thinking of taking up a new hobby or two, but you wouldn't have time if you were doing something else such as going to a sports match, film or some other event.

✂ **CUT ALONG DOTTED LINE**

BANG-A-GONG
PERCUSSION
INSTRUMENTS

Large gongs a speciality

(These make a fantastic Goonnnnnngg! sound)

345 Church Street

119

Cut out and use the doctor's note below:

DOCTOR BROWN THE SURGERY

To whom it may concern:

It is my professional opinion (an opinion which has been honed and shaped by years of expert tuition in a whole variety of medical training establishments and by staying up late to read whopping great technical manuals about medicine) that this child has a rather rare skin complaint.

Although they probably look fine, I would strongly advise that you keep your distance (especially if you are a relation) and don't go kissing them as this may have surprising and disastrous effects.

Yours

Dr

P.S. This is all definitly completely bona fide

CUT ALONG DOTTED LINE

part
eight

Chores

CHORES

W<small>E DECIDED TO GO UNDERCOVER TO RESEARCH</small> chores and how they are done. Of course, at first we didn't know where to go or who to ask, but when we showed that we were prepared to pay good money for information by wearing T-shirts saying: 'We're prepared to pay good money for information', our first contact introduced himself on the top of a bus.

Our contact in the murky world of house-hold chores was known to us only as

Bob
'83 Florence Road,
Finsbury Park,
London, N4 4DP'
Simpkinson.

We had no idea where he came from. He promised us that he could find us a large number of these so-called 'chores' to do, with no questions asked. We paid him

£50,000

in a brown paper envelope and he introduced us to someone he called 'his wife'. We came to know her as

Eileen
'83 Florence Road, etc'
Simpkinson.

For 18 months we did the washing up, vacuuming, polishing and tidying up at their secret address.

It was at this stage that we realised it was all a bit of a con. We left, disgruntled, and with rather a lot of explaining to do to our publishers, Knight Books. We had given them the impression, through hints and half-truths that we hadn't just spent the money.

What we can definitely tell you however is that on the basis of our experience,

CHORES ARE REALLY BAD NEWS AND YOU SHOULD TRY AND AVOID THEM WHEREVER POSSIBLE.

HERE'S HOW

If you are asked to wash up, fill in this letter, cut it out and give it to the relevant adult.

SCHOOL PAPER
for IMPORTANT school letters only

CUT ALONG DOTTED LINE

Dear

     Your child is in charge of the school wormery at the moment and is doing very well. Seldom have we had so many worms, worming around all over the place. It is very important for the wormery, and the school, which is participating in the National Worm League, that this good work continues.

     As you may know, soap and detergents act as an irritant to worms, even if present in the smallest quantities.

     I would therefore ask you not to allow your child near any soap or detergents (especially anything related to washing up) for the time being.

     Best wishes

P.S. Using washing up gloves wouldn't help, for fairly technical reasons.

WASHING UP 2

Homework tonight is to draw one of your family doing the following activities in the space provided:

1 Laying the table

2 Cleaning the table

3 Washing up

4 Still washing up

CUT ALONG DOTTED LINE

Cut out this notice and leave it on the windscreen of the car before you are supposed to wash it.

CUT ALONG DOTTED LINE

POLICE NOTICE

THIS CAR WAS NEAR THE SCENE OF A MAJOR CRIME. THE POLICE MAY NEED TO TEST IT FOR FINGERPRINTS, AND MATCHING FIBRES.

You are hereby notified that this car MUST NOT be cleaned or repainted until further notice.

(Issued pursuant to Schedule 1 of Section 359 of the Police and Criminal Evidence Act 1984.)

WASHING THE CAR 2

Leave this on the windscreen of the car.

✂ **CUT ALONG DOTTED LINE**

Congratulations!

By leaving your car to get this dirty, you must have saved lots of water and not used detergents on it. It is therefore now on the shortlist for our 'ecologically friendly car award' which will be judged on the state of your car in a few weeks, time. You could win £100 if it stays really dirty!

THE GREEN PARTY —

Keeping Britain Dirty

WASHING THE CAR 3

Leave this on the windscreen of the car.

From the

B.B.C.

WOOD LANE SHEPHERD'S BUSH
LONDON

Dear Car Owner,

Your car was mistakenly heavily featured in a scene from the BBC production of John Godber's new play *The Tony Gubba Laughter Café* today.

As we may well wish to feature your car even more prominently in a further scene we request you most earnestly not to wash it, as we are always vigilant to maintain exact continuity, and we don't want tons of people writing into *Points of View* to say we've made a mistake.

Obviously, if we were able to use it, we would certainly pay you a large wodge of dosh.

Yours sincerely

Director General, BBC

WEEDING THE GARDEN 3

1 Cut out the plant name plates below and attach them to small gardening canes.

2 Stick them prominently in any area where there are weeds.

3 Tell your mum or dad that you've identified all the plants in the garden and there is in fact no weeding to be done.

CUT ALONG DOTTED LINE

Rare Plantus

Leave This Herus

Not-to-be-pulled-upus

Not-at-all-a-weedus

No-gardening-needed-herus

Rare Plantus

Leave This Herus

Not-to-be-pulled-upus

Not-at-all-a-weedus

No-gardening-needed-herus

4 A LIST OF EXCUSES FOR HAVING FORGOTTEN TO BUY ONE INGREDIENT AT THE SHOPS

1   I thought it would be a good idea to try the recipe without it.

2 That product has been recently withdrawn after Government health warnings.

3   There was only one left, so I let the very old man who lives on his own have it.

4   I noticed that the packaging was environmentally unfriendly.

5   I suddenly remembered the Norwegian proverb 'Haaden ner fjørden.'

CLEANING YOUR SHOES 1 5

Cut out and stick this label to the tin of shoe polish.

When your parents see your shoes and ask why you haven't cleaned them, present them with the tin.

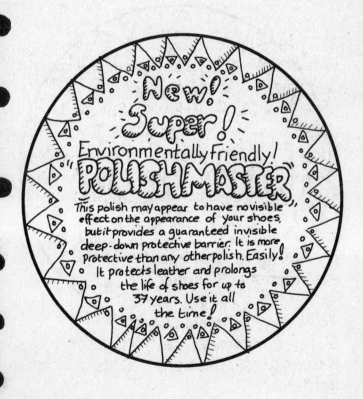

New! Super! Environmentally friendly! "POLISHMASTER"

This polish may appear to have no visible effect on the appearance of your shoes, but it provides a guaranteed invisible deep-down protective barrier. It is more protective than any other polish. Easily! It protects leather and prolongs the life of shoes for up to 37 years. Use it all the time!

CLEANING YOUR SHOES 2

Cut out and stick this label to the tin of shoe polish. Show to your parents, with pride in the way you have avoided spoiling the shoes they bought you.

The Super Duper Rubber Inner
• THE RIGHT WAY TO SHINE •
POLISH

CAUTION: ON NO ACCOUNT, USE THIS POLISH AFTER 1st JANUARY 1992. THIS WILL RUIN ALL KNOWN SHOES FOREVER!

part nine

Staying up late

STAYING UP

PARENTS ARE ALWAYS TRYING TO GET THEIR children into bed at ridiculously early times. This is to be avoided as there may be a good programme on television or you may be deep into a book, or you may have some panel beating to do.*

In our efforts to push back the borders of bedtime, we have recently gained access to government projections relating to life in the future.

(Incidentally, we've also got some 'hot' electrical goods, including televisions with only the screen missing, and a 1989 purple 'Muddy Fox'. Will swop for a Subbuteo team of Hereford United or haberdashery.)

Anyway, these government plans. They show that bedtimes will be very different in the future. In fact, in just 30 years' time, children like you will be allowed to

stay up as late as you want,
to drive,
to go to whatever certificate film you wish
and
not to go to school at all.

* Unlikely this one, to be frank.

This is because in 30 years' time, children like you will be over 40.

There is also a rumour that in the future people will be much taller and wear shock absorbers on their feet, although what that's got to do with staying up late I really have no idea.

EVEN IF YOU'VE NOTHING SPECIFIC TO DO, IT SEEMS SUCH A WASTE TO SPEND ALL THAT TIME

ASLEEP.

<u>For example,</u>

Terry Wogan got to his successful position on just six hours sleep a night. Mind you, he does have ten hours' sleep during the day, and then an hour's nap in the early evening. Honestly, he really is Mr Sleepface.

Anyway, there will obviously be a lot of times when you want to stay up late.

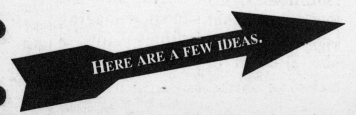

HERE ARE A FEW IDEAS.

1 OFFICIAL REPORT

Cut this out and show it to your parents.

 CUT ALONG DOTTED LINE

TOO MUCH SLEEP IS BAD FOR CHILDREN!

A leading British psychiatr-ist has recently published results of tests which show quite conclusively that too much sleep is bad for children. 'I would say that children should be allowed to stay up late quite often,' he said in a statement today. 'Especially if there's something good on TV.'

Another leading scientist agreed: 'Going to bed early is one of the most damaging things for a child's growth.'

Pau

E

£17
tio
Pri
Hi
•Tt
of £
199
pla
and
•At
lion
busi
dom
enti
•Joh
at D
these
that
the
stat
•An
ment

HOMEWORK 2

Cut out and give this to your parents, after filling in the date of the day you wish to stay up late on. ✂ **CUT ALONG DOTTED LINE**

Dear Parent,

This week, on the _____ (date and time to be filled in after we have contacted the news agencies) a little known **comet** will be passing the earth. This astrological phenomenon will never occur again, and as its existence was first discovered by the headteacher of the school, we ask all parents to allow their children to stay up extra late to view it. It should pass above the area between _____ pm and _____ pm.

We greatly appreciate your cooperation in this as we are doing an important topic on this event, which may well win the school a whole host of whopping great prizes (there may even be a free toast rack in it for you as well if you keep schtum).

Yours

PS Best if your child is fully relaxed to watch the event. Let them watch telly or whatever until late so they're fully prepared in the best possible way.

3 WATCHING THE TV OF YOUR CHOICE

OF COURSE, THERE'S NOT MUCH POINT IN STAYING up if you're forced to sit through boring documentaries or repeats of *Gone Fishing*. To ensure that you get to see the programme of your choice, use the following excuses.

(a) Tune In

Cut out this document and fill in the channel and times of the programme you want to watch. Give it to your parents, saying it was posted through the door earlier. ✂ **CUT ALONG DOTTED LINE**

From Independent and BBC TV Broadcasting Authorities

Important work is to be carried out on the main transmitter in the area this evening. In some places this may well result in your television set only being able to receive channel _____ betweeen the hours of _____ am/pm and _____ am/pm.

Please do not twiddle with the controls or attempt to change channel, as this may cause your television to explode.

We apologise for this slight hiccup in transmission, but at least there's one channel to watch which will no doubt have something brilliant on it.

Yours

(Chief Engineer)

(b) Sleeper

1 Tell your family a week or so in advance that you must never wake a sleep-walker.

2 Pretend to sleep-walk downstairs to the TV just before the programme you want to watch comes on. Turn on the TV and watch the programme, still pretending you are asleep.

3 Deny all knowledge of watching the programme in the morning when your parents quiz you about it.

(c) Homework

Cut out the poem with teacher's comment below and show it to your parents.

✂ **CUT ALONG DOTTED LINE**

SUMMER

The sun shines
Like an upturned butter dish,
Melting its rays on to the wheat
            and barley

Of the mid-western pagoda of life.

9/10 Excellent!
See how this view of
summer relates to tonight's
late film on television.

GENERAL
EMERGENCY

This book has a

BUILT-IN EMERGENCY
SURVIVAL FEATURE:
A CAMOUFLAGE COVER.

If you wish to read this book without a parent or teacher's knowledge, cut out the fake cover on the next page and stick it upside down to the back cover of the book. If you are caught reading this book, you can then simply turn it over and hand it to the adult with the back cover face up.

WORKS

(almost) every time!

Arkwright's Spinning JENNY

A DETAILED HISTORICAL ACCOUNT OF THIS IMPORTANT INVENTION OF THE INDUSTRIAL REVOLUTION. NO FUNNY BITS.

'I hope all children read this. It will make them better behaved and much cleverer.' *Dr Jonathan Miller*

'I think all children should read this pronto.'
Prince Charles

'Marvellous, really marvellous.'
National Union of Teachers

'I wouldn't be at all cross if I caught anyone in my class reading this fantastic book.' *Head Teachers of Eton, Gordonstoun and 47 other prominent British schools*

'Triffic!'   *Mr and Mrs Kenneth Clark*

Cut out
page 142

INSTRUCTIONS
ON PAGE 141

Arkwright's
Spinning
JENNY

A detailed historical account of this
pivotal event of the industrial revolution.

This important book should not be
flicked through but read carefully.
Anyone just flicking through the pages
may become mixed up and irrational.

DO NOT TURN OVER
unless you bought this book or are
under 18 years of age.